Resolution

Solution

2015

3 Easy Steps to Succeed in the New Year

CHRIS WEILER

MythBuster Media Inc
Chicago

Copyright © 2015 by Chris Weiler

Books may be purchased in quantity and/or special sales
by contacting the publisher.

MythBuster Media Inc.
Chicago
sales@MythBusterMedia.com
www.MythBusterMedia.com

Library of Congress Control Number: 2014922594

ISBN 098917963X
ISBN 978-0-9891796-3-8
Cover Design: Gion-Per Marxer - Gion-Per@BeeCoding.com

Contents

Introduction 1

1. Step One - Do This First 3

2. Steps Two and Three - Do These Daily 9

3. Let's Review 17

4. Why We Fail 21

5. Practical Applications 35

Introduction

My objective is to provide you with the most efficient and effective method to succeed in your resolutions this year. To this end I have created a simple 3 step Resolution Solution. In less than 50 pages you will have command over this powerful process to ensure you achieve your New Year's Resolutions.

In most cases, the unmet items on your resolution list exist because you have conditioned reflexive behaviors that oppose your efforts. By following the three actionable steps in this book, you will create new reflexive habits to support succeeding in your resolutions.

Pay close attention to Chapter 4, where you will discover why most people (92%) fail in their resolutions.

I wrote this book as a lean and efficient guide for the *just tell me what to do, make it easy* and *make it work* crowd. If you want a very detailed, in-depth breakdown on how to achieve goals, get my book *The Reflex - Activate Thoughts, Words and Actions to Achieve Your Goals.*

Quick note about myself. I am a performance expert to athletes, Fortune 500's and occasionally, the hoi polloi.

Let's Do It!

Chapter 1

Step One - Do This First

The first and most crucial step is to create a **Guiding Principle**. Simply state a concept, ideal or way of being that directly or indirectly anchors you to your resolution. **Guiding Principle**s are best expressed as value driven statements such as Family First, Education First, Health First, Patience, Compassion, How Can I Serve You, or Pay it Forward. A **Guiding Principle** represents a priority in your life, enabling the empowerment of both yourself and others.

Principles are what you believe and put your faith in. They provide a lens to focus and express your actions through. Principles shape how you perceive yourself, other people, circumstances and the world around you.

Guiding Principles keep your *attention* on your *intention*, by keeping you focused on what is required to support your resolution. Think of your **Guiding Principle** as a bridge enabling you to transport your resolution from inception to completion. Without this bridge, you must rely on willpower or short term inspiration and momentum, which rarely have the capacity to achieve lasting change.

Personally, I visualize driving a stake or flag into the ground to represent my principles. This imagery plants a fixed point of reference in my mind and heart, with the power to create and attract thoughts, words and actions to support those principles.

Having your first child is an example of a fixed point in one's life. Most people take this opportunity to define principles of how they will act as parents to guide their child's development.

The nature of a child, to be dependent on others to survive, when aligned with the parent's **Guiding Principles**, automatically attracts a lifestyle in the form of thoughts, words and actions to support their **Guiding Principles**, while at the same time eliminating things that oppose these values. It then follows, we begin to struggle when we do not have practices in place to help create thoughts, words and actions that align with our principles.

Create Your Guiding Principle

Now that you understand the value and power of **Guiding Principle**s - choose one. What is your fixed point of reference that will help attract thoughts, words and actions to stay the course in achieving your resolutions? Don't worry about choosing a perfect one, as you can always modify it later. For now simply go with your reflex. What is your first thought or feeling that is triggered when asked to choose a **Guiding Principle**? Write down your **Guiding Principle** - Now.

Serves Many Masters

Guiding Principles are not mutually exclusive from one another. One principle can serve different objectives depending on whether they are directly or indirectly applied.

For example, a direct application of the Family First principle can mean your direct objective is to prioritize the needs of your family, such as being a better listener, financial provider, or spending more time together. Used indirectly however, a Family First principle can help prioritize your weight loss, health or fitness goals. In your heart and mind, simply associate how your personal goal benefits your family by placing your *attention* on the *intention* of your **Guiding Principle** and resolution.

This means financial, fitness or weight loss resolutions can support a resolution to show more patience and compassion to one's family. Losing weight and getting fit, directly help you look, feel and move better in your daily life. Reduced stress, increased energy and better sleep are additional ways you benefit. When you feel good within yourself, you feel happy. Your happiness enables you to create thoughts, words and actions that indirectly support your Family First values. The direct benefits you receive by achieving your weight loss and getting fit resolution, also increases your capacity to give to your family.

Every thought, word and action we create either supports or opposes our **Guiding Principle**s and therefore, resolutions. When faced with an opportunity to choose between that which supports or opposes your efforts, put your *attention* on the object of your *intention*, your **Guiding Principle** and resolution. From the previous example, this means you place your *attention* on your *intention* to support your Family First **Guiding Principle**. This crucial step is the missing link to resolution success. Each time your thoughts, words and actions support your **Guiding Principle**, you make deposits to your behavioral bank account, making it easier to withdraw the funds that support those habits the next time, moving you one step closer to resolution victory.

Intention

Guiding Principles are driven by purposeful intention. Without the focused intention of a purpose, you are detached from what you feel and believe in your heart - your Authentic Self. If you only care about the benefits of a goal and not the process required to achieve it, then you lack the required intention to support, drive and motivate you to endure the process. Said another way, when your heart does not *feel like* there is any purpose to the process, your resolution efforts become *half-hearted*. When you struggle with your thoughts, words and actions in support of your resolution, it is because you have not established a **Guiding Principle** to plug your purposeful intent into. Therefore, failure is likely as you are subject to whatever reflexive responses are tied to your existing habits and behaviors.

Emotion Creates *Motion*

Motivation cannot be acquired externally, but must be developed from within, when we are emotionally *moved* or inspired. Without a value driven **Guiding Principle**, your resolutions become solely benefits driven (what you will get at the end), which is why you lack the motivation to see your resolutions through. Of course we all want the benefits, but keeping your attention and your heart on the principles and values those benefits are tied to, is what distinguishes those who fail from those who succeed.

Buddhists say, change and fulfillment only occur when we move what we think from the level of our head down to our heart. The idea may start in the mind, but until it is mixed with your heart, your emotions, how you feel, it lacks the required power to create meaningful, lasting change or fulfillment. Said another way, *emotion creates motion.*

Use Your Religion

For those of you who are religious, incorporate your religion in your **Guiding Principle**. Get organized, lose weight, address your finances, find love or put your relationships first by creating thoughts, words and actions that better enable you to help others in the name of your religious tenets. Specifically, put your *attention* on taking daily actionable steps that move you closer to your resolution, with the *intention* that success in your goal will allow you to better express your religious values.

When the religious beliefs in your heart, couple with the resolutions in your head, they immaculately conceive an offspring that empowers you to achieve your goals and better support your religious principles.

To be clear, I do not generally support or oppose using religion in crafting your **Guiding Principle**. What I specifically support is what is important to you, what YOU value, in your heart. If it is religion, wonderful - use it. If not, also wonderful - use something else.

Reality Check

Resolutions are NOT achieved directly. They are indirect by-products of your daily habits and rituals - your lifestyle. **Guiding Principles** keep you connected to a value driven lifestyle capable of achieving your resolutions.

For those of you still procrastinating on creating a **Guiding Principle**, do it now. You will need it for the final two steps, which we will cover next.

Chapter 2

Steps Two and Three - Do These Daily

We are what we repeatedly do.
Excellence, then, is not an act, but a habit. - Aristotle

In this chapter we will uncover the two daily action steps that will create a bridge between your **Guiding Principle** and resolution. Much like the objective of bumper bowling, where guiderails keep your ball out of the gutter, assuring you hit at least one pin, these two actions serve as behavior guiderails, assuring you keep on track to fulfill your resolutions.

1. Check Your Mind

Discover what you think and feel when you are conflicted between doing something that opposes rather than supports your resolution.

How it Works

This is performed silently, so it can be done anywhere, anytime. Simply **Check Your Mind** to discover what you think and feel at any given moment, but especially when you feel stressed or conflicted between thoughts, words and actions that do not support your resolution. Be honest, as there is no right or wrong answer. Personally, I check my mind throughout the day while driving, writing, during conversation and shopping.

Perhaps you are trying to diet and know you should be following a proper nutrition model, like the one found in my nutrition book **The 3/4 Rule**. However, you are craving foods that don't support or will sabotage your diet goals. This is the time to **Check Your Mind** and discover the thoughts and feelings that drive and nourish those cravings. Whatever thoughts and feelings you discover - name them.

The next step is to decide if you like what you think or feel. Again, no wrong or right answer, simply what is right or wrong for YOU. Perhaps you have been eating a balanced diet and meeting your exercise goals for the past 3 weeks. So, you **Check Your Mind** and discover that you feel pretty good about your craving for that 600 calorie dessert. However, if you don't feel good about it, yet still submit to your craving, you are reinforcing habits that may sabotage your efforts and set you up for failure. You cannot simply rely on an intellectual justification, as the power lies in how you *feel*, and you need to *feel good* about it. This is how we unite the Mind, Body and Heart, and condition them to best support our future efforts.

Whenever you **Check Your Mind** and discover you do not like what you think or feel, name a thought or feeling that opposes it, and supports the thoughts, feelings and reflexive habits you want to reinforce. This simply requires you conduct yourself in a way that reflects the thoughts, words and actions you want to develop.

For example, let's imagine I have just finished eating all the food on my plate while at a family holiday meal, and reflexively ready to get a second serving. However, I stop to **Check My Mind** and discover although I feel like eating more, as I am conditioned to associate food with increasing my happiness and satisfaction while socializing, I am conflicted and therefore do not feel good about my actions opposing my **Guiding Principle** and resolution. I attempt to justify my actions with internal dialogue such as, *It's the holidays, I'm with family and friends, I want to feel free to enjoy myself and not feel restricted for just one day.* I can justify my actions with every logically persuasive argument available, and yet none of it is relevant if I do not feel good about my actions. When I take action, yet do not feel good about it, I fracture the foundation that supports my efforts at achieving my goals. Repeated fractures will destroy my goals.

In this instance I can create thoughts and feelings that support my resolution by placing my *attention* on my *intention* to acquire these same unrestricted feelings of enjoyment I normally associate with food, by engaging with others and focusing on their needs. Did you catch the subtle, yet powerful shift that just occurred? The shift happened when I took the attention off myopically satisfying my own needs, which for some reason require food to fulfill, and focusing on the needs of others. The type and quantity of bio-chemicals produced are different when focused inwardly on myself, than when externally focused on others. The power of this bio-chemical shift disengages the flow of chemicals nourishing my habits that oppose my goals.

There is no universal right or wrong answer, just what is right or wrong for you. This means you could be sitting at the table with me in my holiday meal example, and share my exact same resolution, yet it is okay for me to get a second serving, while it is not the correct action for you. What each of us privately thinks and feels need to be in alignment or we will fail in our resolutions.

From productivity at work, to communication issues with family, friends, co-workers, bosses or employees, to challenges with anger, stress or depression, to problems with personal finance, **Checking Your Mind** will unveil the subconscious triggers that disrupt your ability to put your *attention* on the *intention* of your **Guiding Principle**. **Checking Your Mind** enables you to successfully navigate the path to your resolution's destination.

Why it Works

We need to synchronize our habits and actions with what is written in our subconscious minds. If there is not a script that reflexively cues you to take action in support of your goals, failure becomes more likely. **Checking Your Mind** breaks your reflexive response pattern. This action increases the gap between moments, and the interval between one reflexive response and another. Questioning how you think and feel, requires you to be present and in the moment, enabling you to uncover and address the root of your self-sabotaging behavior.

Understand that **Checking Your Mind** is both about how you think and feel. You might only be aware of what you think in a given moment, but recognize there is always an emotion tied to your thought. Some of you will need to dig deeper than others to root it out.

2. Compose Yourself

The final step of our Resolution Success model is a simple writing exercise designed to remove subconscious barriers that oppose your resolutions, while creating the causes for thoughts, words and actions in support of your resolutions.

How it Works

With 2-3 blank sheets of paper, begin writing as fast as you can whatever is in your head. DO NOT judge, worry about grammar, punctuation, legibility or try to make it about anything specific. This is a free flow, subconscious mind dump, from your head to paper. Curse, be profane, prolific, happy, angry, sad or silly. Let whatever is in you flow uninterrupted from pen to paper. Feel free to begin by writing how weird you think this exercise is. What you write does not need to make sense, and might look or feel like inane ramblings - it's all good! When finished, shred or file your writing and move on with your day.

Although you can **Compose Yourself** anytime, it has a more profound impact immediately after waking in the morning, before you interface with any person or technology. This means before email, phone or TV.

You heard me, BEFORE email or phone. Close your eyes and take a breath - you can do it!

Why it Works

This is a daily, subconscious house cleaning, that first brings awareness, then helps loosen and remove the harmful deposits in your subconscious mind. These damaging deposits create and reinforce habits that contribute to poor performance. You see, the conscious mind references the subconscious mind for most of our conscious actions.

Our past and current thoughts, words and actions are deposited in the subconscious mind. These deposits are reflexively used to shape our future Thoughts, Words and Actions. Much like a checking account, whatever deposits have been made, are what is available for withdrawal.

A Bit More on Composing Yourself

Ideally, you should always shoot for 3 pages. It often requires this amount of space and time to go deep enough to loosen the entrenched thoughts and deeply embedded baggage deposited in your subconscious mind. At times however, you may be genuinely done after 2 pages, and have nothing else to write. There are also times when you are short on time and simply need to stop. That's okay, as the process of changing behaviors and habits is an endurance event, NOT a sprint.

Feel proud and satisfied you took the few moments you had to **Compose Yourself**, rather than justify blowing it off because something else came up, and you plan to *do it later*. Of course there are times when this will happen, so **Check Your Mind** to honestly distinguish between your legitimate and illegitimate reasons.

Action Steps

Another, powerful way to **Compose Yourself**, which goes beyond a *subconscious house cleaning*, is to integrate action steps. Action steps are bridges that connect thoughts, goals and plans to their manifestation in reality.

Sure, you have plans to save money, quit smoking, stop procrastinating, get married, get divorced, start your business or lose weight. So, what actionable steps have you taken to bridge the gap between your schemes, dreams, and desired outcome?

FIRST

Check Your Mind to discover what you think or feel when you are stressed, angry, depressed, aren't being productive, procrastinating, or experiencing any thoughts, words or actions that oppose your goals. There is no right or wrong answer, simply an honest unveiling of the subconscious triggers that create obstacles between you and your happiness.

SECOND

Name the thoughts and/or feelings and write them down on a piece of paper. Be Concise, choosing as few words as possible.

THIRD

Choose one or more words that counter or oppose the thoughts and feelings you wrote above and write them down.

FOURTH

Building Bridges. Write down ONE action step that physically connects you to your goal and moves you one step closer to integrating it into your life. Ex. Sign up for class. Get up and run a 1/4 mile. Make that call. Now write this action step over and over until you fill up the page. When finished, get up and do it - NOW!

Repeat the process tomorrow with another action step. Adding a pebble a day to a jar at first seems insignificant, but the cumulative effect is quickly recognized.

Why This Works

This version of **Compose Yourself** adds the additional element of **Action Steps**. Since many of us get bogged down at this critical juncture between thought and action, this exercise enables us to successfully bridge the gap. The cumulative effect of taking small, seemingly insignificant daily actions is the secret to great accomplishments.

Chapter 3

Let's Review

Create a value-driven, **Guiding Principle** that will help attract thoughts, words and actions enabling you to stay the course in achieving your resolutions.

Check Your Mind to discover what you think and feel about any thoughts, words or actions that relate to your resolution. Decide if they support or oppose your resolution. Do you feel - good or bad? If you don't feel good, name the thought and feeling you would like to replace it with and perform some action that supports and expresses that thought and feeling.

Compose Yourself. With 2-3 blank sheets of paper, begin writing as fast as you can whatever is in your head. DO NOT judge, worry about grammar, punctuation, legibility or try to make it about anything specific. This is a free flow, subconscious mind dump, from your head to paper. Shred your writing or file it for future reference, the choice is yours.

Compose Yourself with Action Steps.

a. Name and write down the feelings and thoughts discovered when you **Checked Your Mind**. Be concise, choosing as few words as possible.

b. Choose one or more words that oppose those thoughts and feelings and write them down.

c. Write down ONE action step that physically connects you to your resolution and moves you one step closer to integrating it into your lifestyle. As fast as possible, write this action step over and over until you fill the page. Get up and perform that action step - NOW!

d. Repeat this process as needed to stay the course.

Weight loss, health, fitness, finances, education, relationship and mental/emotional resolutions are all governed by one common element - conditioned reflexes. You see, the conscious mind references the subconscious mind to produce the majority of one's thoughts, words and actions. Good or bad, whatever you have deposited into your subconscious mind, is what is reflexively available for the conscious mind to withdraw.

Understanding that the circular relationship between the conscious and subconscious mind is similar to a checking account, dependent on a system of deposits and withdrawals, helps demystify the interplay between these parts of the brain.

As with a physical checking account, the funds available for withdrawal are dependent on the funds that have been deposited. People who succeed in their resolutions, make deposits to their subconscious, capable of producing behaviors that support their objectives. Those who fail, simply make deposits that oppose their efforts.

Every thought you generate, word you speak and action you take, either supports or opposes your resolution success, as a non-effect cannot exist. **Checking Your Mind** and **Composing Yourself** keep you anchored to your **Guiding Principle**s and achieving what is important to you in life.

Chapter 4

Why We Fail

We are what we repeatedly do.
Excellence, then, is not an act, but a habit. - Aristotle

Aristotle's quote is as relevant here as it is in Chapter 2, which is why it is repeated. Resolutions are NOT achieved directly. They are indirect by-products of your daily habits and rituals - your lifestyle. The problem is that we are creatures of immediate gratification with magic-bullet mentalities. We are seduced by quick fixes, sound-bite advice and solutions provided in 140 characters or less. While these abbreviated actions may give us the illusory perception we are keeping pace with the social currency of the day, it also makes those solutions cheap, disposable and therefore, not valuable or helpful in meeting our resolutions.

To help you avoid the common obstacles that interfere with achieving your goals, this chapter will uncover the four most toxic, yet subtle elements that destroy our resolution resolve.

Reason #1 - Consumerism

I am comfortable saying, *consumerism is the root of all resolution evil*, as the other reasons given in this chapter that create obstacles on your resolution highway, all stem from *consumerism*.

The Short Explanation:

- We suffer from consumerism.

- When not consuming, we spend the majority of our waking hours planning what to consume and acquiring that which enables us to consume (work/money).

- As such, most of us look at ourselves, other people and life in general, through the filtered eyes of a consumer.

- We the consumer have been conditioned to search outside of the mind, body and heart, within the consumer market, for solutions to both personal goals and societal problems. This approach often fails, as consumer goods and services are rarely capable of inspiring us to *feel like* taking the necessary steps to achieve our goals.

- When your heart and mind are in alignment, they create motivation, desire and passion, empowering you to stay the course until you reach your goals. This is the secret to fulfilling your resolutions. The consumer market cannot give you this, as motivation, desire and passion cannot be consumed or acquired through external sources.

The Longer Explanation:

The majority of people are conditioned from birth to be consumers. In fact, while being resold the American Dream, our post World War II government made it clear the primary duty of an American was to be a consumer. Not surprising when you consider the fiscal toll that war took on our economy.

However, our conditioned consumer habits often oppose personally meaningful goals and resolutions. The inherent problem is that resolutions, often enmeshed with personal development and happiness, cannot be acquired through *consumerism*. Contrary to their marketing claims, you cannot lose weight, get fit, find love, quit smoking or improve your finances through the consumption of goods and services, until both your head and heart are in alignment. Your heart creates the motivation to drive the resolutions in your head to completion. The consumer market attempts to bypass this head/heart relationship by convincing you to purchase a readymade solution to achieve your resolution. *Consumerism is simply the wrong tool for the job.*

As with any tool, consumer goods and services have no power to give you anything until acted upon by YOU. Your mind, heart, intention and skill all determine whether you use your hammer to build something wonderful or destroy something beautiful. Common consumer tools to help our resolutions include to join a club, hire a trainer, start a new fad diet, sign up for online dating or slap on that nicotine patch. Oh... and buy books like the one you are reading now.

Sure, come January you can follow the rest of the weight loss resolution herd into fitness centers and health clubs across the nation. Your short lived motivation will last until about February, when the herd retreats back to their familiar, non-exercise habits. The regulars at the gym will say to each other, *glad that's over until next January* (actual quote), and appreciate having their uncrowded gym back.

The point is, until you have done the internal work, such as develop a **Guiding Principle** and reinforce its use by **Checking Your Mind** and **Composing Yourself**, you may not have the capacity, drive and motivation to use your consumer tools in a way that will ensure you succeed in your resolutions.

To be clear, this is not an indictment on capitalism. However, it is important to understand how our conditioned consumer reflexes often conflict with our goals.

Many people find this distinction difficult as they have only looked at the world through the eyes of a consumer. We spend the majority of our first 25 years of life, being pushed through an educational system that was primarily constructed for one purpose - to get a job. From the economy's perspective, our jobs serve the distinct function of enabling our ability to purchase and consume goods and services, which are *supposed to make us happy*. You know, the white picket fence and so forth.

Since the marketplace exists to buy and sell, it can only define happiness in context of its architecture - acquisition and consumption - thereby reinforcing its own existence and needs. What about your personal needs, thoughts and feelings that transcend the limitations of the latest version of a product or service?

Are most of these goods and services relevant and valuable in context of your Authentic Self, what you personally require to be happy or achieve your goals? How would you know? The consumer marketing machine is only concerned with satisfying your Consumer Self, the result of which has conditioned a set of wants and needs that do not necessarily reflect the needs and wants of your Authentic Self.

The misalignment between one's Authentic Self and Consumer Self are where most people's resolution efforts get derailed. The consumer marketplace has created a list of items for you to choose from when making your how to have a happy life checklist, which typically includes the right job, house, spouse, kids, zip code, car, clothing, appearance, personal accessories and technology. The question begged, do my choices in these areas support my Authentic Self or my Consumer Self?

Although we are conditioned to relate to everything we see in terms of consumption, goals and happiness are processes that require development, and development cannot be acquired solely by consumption of goods and services. The marketplace simply does not and cannot sell what is required to achieve these things unless you honestly have a passionate connection to those goods and services that inspires motivation.

The most important areas of lives, where we spend the most time, money and effort, require years of development including relationships, education, occupation, personal and physical growth. It then follows and comes as no surprise, those who try to shortcut or bypass development, typically fail in achieving their goals.

The *thing* Has No Power - You Do!

Have you ever wondered why some people succeed in their resolutions, while others fail, yet they use the exact same consumer driven product or service? As is true with any tool, the diet, gym, fitness app, dating service, or self-help book, have little power to give you anything until powered by YOU. **The *thing* Has No Power - You Do**, is what distinguishes those who attain their resolutions from those who do not, and reinforces the point of this book: To achieve your resolution, empower it with a **Guiding Principle**, as this is what creates motivation to succeed. Unless the truth is, you honestly *don't feel like it*. We will address this next.

Reason #2 - I Don't Feel Like It

Emotion creates *motion*. This means we are motivated to take action on what we feel or *feel like* doing. When what we think about our resolution is in alignment with how we feel about our resolution, we succeed. It then follows, failure occurs when what we think and feel are not in alignment. The primary reason people do not succeed in their resolutions...

They simply *don't feel like it*.

Our basic rational for why we do or do not do something, has not changed much from when we were 5 years old. When we are young and don't want to do something, we simply say, *I don't wanna!* When pressed further for an answer, we have one additional layer of introspection available by explaining, because *I don't feel like it*.

Regardless of our age, the reality is that mostly we do something because we *feel like it*, or don't do something because we *don't feel like it*.

Sure, some of you are thinking, I do plenty of things I *don't feel like* doing including work, school, household and family obligations. Take a moment and reflect on your daily responsibilities and obligations, the things you feel you do for others. Part of this list will undoubtedly include things you *don't feel like* doing, but do anyway.

With this in mind, I challenge you to explain why you do these things, without using the words *I, ME, MY, OUR,* or including any physical, mental or emotional benefit to yourself. You will find this a nearly impossible task.

You might not *feel like* working, but you do so because you *feel like* receiving the benefits it provides for yourself and the people you care about. As parents, we are often in the position of doing things we *don't feel like* doing. I *don't feel like* driving my daughter to her friends house, spending six hours at a gymnastics meet, track meet, choir concert, violin recital or attending team and school fundraisers.

I do however, *feel like* supporting one of my **Guiding Principles,** to aid in the development of a compassionate, happy, healthy, thinking person, that I love with all my heart. So when she asks me to drive her to a friends house, I put my *attention* on my **Guiding Principle,** with the *intention* of contributing to my daughters happiness and healthy social development. The result is an alignment of my thoughts, words and actions with my **Guiding Principle,** which enables me to *feel like* driving her. Said another way, I put my *attention* on my love for her, which creates feelings that motivate me to take action. This is a very different dynamic, which produces very different feelings, than simply supporting my daughter out of reflexive duty and obligation.

In case you missed it, the paragraph above explains exactly how to apply **Guiding Principles** and integrate them into your heart and mind. Please re-read.

Weight Loss

Unless you have a metabolic, physical, or hormonal disorder, or limited by certain prescription medication, you lose weight because you want to lose weight. Conversely, if you cannot lose weight and maintain it, you simply *don't feel like it* - enough. As I said, emotion creates motion, and we are motivated to take action when we *feel like it*.

That's right, I said if you cannot lose weight, and keep a personally acceptable amount off long term, then you honestly do not want to achieve your weight loss goals bad enough. More specifically, you are not emotionally invested enough to *feel* sufficiently motivated to alter or create a lifestyle that supports your goal. Sure, you want the end result, the benefits, but not bad enough to put in the required effort. You also might enjoy the benefits of owning your own business, but are you willing to do what is necessary to achieve that end?

Most people are not, which is why there will always be another fat loss *tip, trick* or *hack* available for your consumption. Simply put, most people who do not succeed in their resolutions *don't feel like* doing what is necessary to achieve results. If your weight loss resolution is primarily benefits driven, meaning to receive compliments, fit into certain clothes and improve your social currency, you will likely fail.

Benefits that solely feed your ego, rarely have the power to create sustained motivation unless you feel very passionately about those benefits. The narcissists who prioritize how they look over everything else in life succeed because they live by a **Guiding Principle** of aesthetics. Remember, **Guiding Principle**s do not have to be *principled*. Passion perseveres!

The more passionately you feel about something, the more likely your success - good or bad. Consider how passionate terrorists are about their ends. The point is, resolution success happens when your feelings are in alignment with your thoughts, words and actions, thus producing the required motivation to see it through to completion.

Reason #3 - Tips, Tricks and Hacks

Our love affair with *tips, tricks* and *hacks* (shortcuts), is another phenomenon that powerfully contributes to our struggles with habits and behaviors that oppose our resolution efforts.

Nearly every day I receive requests to provide *tips, tricks* and *hacks (shortcuts)* for fitness, weight loss, nutrition, fear, stress, motivation, mindfulness, procrastination and productivity. Three months ago I received one asking for tips on how to be happy in 10 minutes or less. Really!? As if happiness were a light switch to be turned on and off at will, or by pressing a few buttons. Rather, it is the indirect by-product of specific thoughts, words and actions expressed over time that contribute to the development of general happiness and achieving our goals.

I recently received a request for *tips* and *tricks* on how to have *The Talk* with your kids. If you have not had the foresight, and taken the effort to develop general bridges of communication with your children from day one, it will not be there for you to cross when you want to drive *The Talk* vehicle across. For those of you who say, *my kids won't talk to me*, re-read the previous sentence.

What happens when our addiction to shortcuts, couples with the wants, desires and goals of our conditioned consumer mindset? Well, they produce offspring that are reflexively susceptible to *tips, tricks* and *hacks*.

Learn this one trick to lose belly fat.

Tips on how to score. (Maybe I'm talking sports, maybe not).

Tips on how to get organized and save money.

5 tips to improve motivation.

5 tips to decrease procrastination.

Tips, tricks and *hacks* exist to beat stress, be happy, find love, make up, break up, stop smoking, eat less, earn more, lose weight, get ripped, reduce wrinkles... and the list goes on.

I know, YOU are never seduced by these pitches - I'm talking about *other people*. While reading the examples above, you are removed from the event and can therefore look at them objectively, with a rational mind, and convince yourself *I'd never fall for that!* Yet, from within the situation, in the heat of the moment, the rational centers of the brain soften.

Tips, tricks and hacks are the perfect vehicle to entice the conditioned mind of your Consumer Self, to purchase products and services that look and sound great, but rarely have any value at addressing the goals and resolutions of your Authentic Self. Once you wipe the slick layers of marketing goo off your the product or service that is supposed to help you achieve your resolutions, you are simply left with a tool that requires YOU to power it to achieve anything.

Reason #4 - <u>Value Driven vs. Benefits Driven</u>

Many people who struggle with their resolutions are not truly interested in the goal itself. They simply want the BENEFITS of being organized, spending less, saving more, losing weight, quitting smoking or falling in love - 6 of the top 10 resolutions in 2014.

Sure, most people want the benefits of being wealthy or fit, but are not sufficiently motivated to *take* the steps required to achieve those benefits. This distinction is why lifestyle movements such as paleo-diets are more successful than not, while producing loyalty and lifestyle integration similar to religious movements. Contrary to popular belief, the magic does not lie in the types of foods they eat, but belief in the value driven principles of a lifestyle built on respecting the health and fitness of their body. In turn, this leads to choices that support their **Guiding Principle** of living a healthy and fit lifestyle.

As such, paleo-enthusiasts are not primarily focused on the benefits driven goal of fitting into a pair of skinny jeans, receiving peer approval or increasing one's social currency. Instead, they are often driven by health and fitness goals to improve how they function personally and professionally. Looking better is often a welcome by-product.

Value driven goals create thoughts, words and actions necessary to support the objective. Not valuing the goal emotionally disconnects you from it - *your heart's not in it*. This brings us back full circle to the immense power of **Guiding Principle**s, as they are what keeps us emotionally connected to our daily actions. **Guiding Principle**s keep you anchored to a value driven lifestyle capable of achieving your resolutions.

The question is, do you value the goal or simply value the benefits and social currency the marketplace and society value at that moment?

Check Your Mind!

Chapter 5

Applications

In this chapter I will show you how to apply the advice in this book to the top 3 resolutions of 2014, using the same **Guiding Principle** for each one. In this way, I will demonstrate how these seemingly separate areas of our lives are really all connected at the level of the heart. Recognizing this connection should empower you with a perspective that greatly simplifies achieving any personally meaningful goal.

Top 3 Resolutions of 2014

1. Lose Weight
2. Get Organized
3. Spend Less / Save More

Lose Weight - Step One

Construct a **Guiding Principle**, a value driven statement that reflects an emotional connection to your goal. In each of our examples I will assign the following **Guiding Principle**, "respect and love for myself and family."

Aside from yourself, who do you care about that would benefit from your losing weight? It is important to distinguish between those who you don't care about, yet would benefit, from those you do care about and would also benefit. Simply including your spouse, children, significant other or siblings because they are family, and therefore believe you should include them in the circle of people you care about, but do not in context of your goal, will likely result in resolution failure.

Alignment between what you think and feel is the single most important factor in succeeding in personally meaningful goals. You need to honestly and authentically care about the person in context of your resolution, not say you care because you are supposed to or because of their title. Be honest, as there is no right or wrong in this context, simply what is right or wrong for you. If what you feel or don't feel is an expression of your Authentic Self, then it has to be right for you, in this moment.

What is built into this declaration is an emotional anchor point rooted in how you feel about and value yourself, and those you love. For some of you, *family* extends beyond blood or marital relationships to include close friends. Remember, *emotion creates motion*, so the most important factor is how you *feel* about them, not their title.

Now consider how losing weight will improve how you feel and enhance how you look, while increasing energy, decreasing stress and creating more ease of movement in your daily activities.

Next, reflect on how these personal changes within you will add value and increase the level of happiness in the lives of the people you have connected to your **Guiding Principle**. For example, less stress means more patience for your children and an opportunity for them to model your behavior.

The circle is now complete. You have created a self-reinforcing principle that will attract thoughts, words and actions to support your weight loss resolution efforts.

Lose Weight - Step Two

Compose Yourself. Ideally make this the first thing you do each day, before interfacing with technology or other people. You will need 3 sheets of blank paper for this exercise. On the first 2 blank sheets of paper, begin writing as fast as you can whatever is in your head. DO NOT judge, worry about grammar, punctuation, legibility or try to make it about anything specific. This is a free flow, subconscious mind dump, from your head to paper. Curse, be profane, prolific, happy, angry, sad or silly. Let whatever is in you flow uninterrupted from pen to paper. What you write does not need to make sense, and might look or feel like inane ramblings - it's all good!

With the 3rd sheet of paper, write your resolution, *Lose Weight*. Under your resolution write your **Guiding Principle**. Fill up the page alternating your resolution and **Guiding Principle**. As you do this, hold the image in your mind of the people whose lives will be improved (including you) and how your weight loss success will feel.

So, your **Guiding Principle** aligns your goal with your heart - *emotion creates motion*. **Composing Yourself** serves three purposes. First, the "subconscious mind dump" helps remove reflexive behaviors in your subconscious that oppose your weight loss efforts. Second, it enables deposits to your subconscious that support the foundational habits of weight loss. Third, it provides reinforcement of daily thoughts, words and actions to support your resolution.

Let's look at another potent way to **Compose Yourself.** Write on a blank sheet of paper one action step that moves you one step closer to your weight loss goal. You will either perform this action immediately, or write down what time you will perform it that day. Now re-write your action step over and over, as fast as you can, until you reach the bottom of the page. If performing immediately, get up and do it - NOW! Example actions steps can include signing up for an exercise class or program, getting up and jogging a quarter mile, or fixing a balanced, nutrient dense meal following the simple model in my nutrition book **The 3/4 Rule** (@Amazon).

This is a powerful method that results in the subconscious prioritizing actions to support your resolution and **Guiding Principle**. Done first thing in the morning ensures your first thoughts, words and actions support your goals, before you focus on the rest of your day, which often include actions that oppose your efforts. Having said that, you can also perform this exercise anytime you feel conflicted between your goal and a habit or response that does not support your goal. You discover these opposing forces when you **Check Your Mind.**

Lose Weight - Step Three

The last component of your resolution success model is to **Check Your Mind** - often. This action will keep you from getting lost, as you travel towards your weight loss destination. As with any journey where you consistently check directions to ensure you are getting closer to your destination, **Checking Your Mind** should be the most often used tool throughout the day.

- When constructing your **Guiding Principle**, **Check Your Mind** to discover what and who you honestly think and feel is important.

- **Check Your Mind** to separate your Authentic Self from your Consumer Self.

- In any given moment, do my thoughts, words and actions support or oppose me losing weight and the values of my **Guiding Principle? Check Your Mind!**

- **Check Your Mind** to discover how you feel when you do not want to exercise or eat food that does not support your ends. There are times when you will honestly feel fine about it and should. Although you can attempt to justify actions that oppose your goals until the, but if you do not feel good about your thoughts, your heart and mind will be out of alignment, which will undermine your success.

Your Resolution Success Model

The imagery you should have in your mind is a self-sustaining circle of success, driven and nourished by **Guiding Principles**, **Composing Yourself** and **Checking Your Mind.**

Get Organized - Step One

Remember, we will recycle our **Guiding Principle** used for weight loss to getting organized - "respect and love for myself and family."

Aside from yourself, who do you care about that would benefit from you being better organized? Keep in mind, alignment between what you think and feel is the single most important factor in succeeding in personally meaningful goals. You need to honestly and authentically care about the people involved. Be honest, as there is no right or wrong in this context, simply what is right or wrong for you. If what you feel or don't feel is an expression of your Authentic Self, then it has to be right for you, in this moment.

Consider that a goal to get organized could have immense value to your personal or business goals of helping others. If so, this becomes integrated into the **Guiding Principle** of who and what you respect and love. To be clear, feel free to create any **Guiding Principle** you can imagine, I am merely demonstrating that the true power of a **Guiding Principle** is what it is supported by, which is anchored to what is in your heart and mind.

Now think about how being organized will improve the way you feel, decrease stress and create greater ease of movement in your daily activities. Next, reflect on how these personal changes within you will add value and increase the level of happiness in the lives of the people you have connected to your **Guiding Principle**. The circle is now complete. You have created a self-reinforcing principle that will attract thoughts, words and actions to support your *get organized* resolution.

Caution! Many people do not succeed in these types of resolutions because they merely want the benefits of weight loss, being organized or improving their financial situation. Those whose resolutions are primarily benefit driven mostly fail, as it is difficult to develop the emotional connection that supports the daily action steps required to succeed. Only caring about the benefits, often disconnects you from *feeling like* taking the steps needed to acquire the benefits.

Get Organized - Step Two

Compose Yourself. You will need 3 sheets of blank paper for this exercise. On the first 2 blank sheets of paper, follow the general instructions for **Composing Yourself** previously outlined numerous times in this book.

With the 3rd sheet of paper, write your resolution, *Get Organized*. Under your resolution write your **Guiding Principle** - "respect and love for myself and family." Fill up the page alternating your resolution and **Guiding Principle**.

As you do this, hold the image in your mind of the people whose lives will be improved (including you) and how that will feel when you are organized. Also consider how your daily victories will feel as a result of having taken actionable steps to support your goal.

So, your **Guiding Principle** aligns your goal with your heart - *emotion creates motion*. **Composing Yourself** serves three purposes. First, the "subconscious mind dump" helps remove reflexive behaviors in your subconscious that oppose you getting organized. Second, it enables deposits to your subconscious that support the foundational habits of being organized. Third, it provides reinforcement of daily thoughts, words and actions to support how being organized improves efficiency in all areas of your life.

Let's look at another potent way to **Compose Yourself**. Write on a blank sheet of paper one action step to move you one step closer to an organized life. You will either perform this action immediately, or write down what time you will perform it that day. Now re-write your action step over and over, as fast as you can, until you reach the bottom of the page. If performing immediately, get up and do it - NOW!

This is a powerful method that results in the subconscious prioritizing actions to support your resolution and **Guiding Principle**. Done first thing in the morning ensures your first thoughts, words and actions support your goals, before you focus on the rest of your day, which are typically actions that oppose your efforts.

Having said that, you can also perform this exercise anytime you feel conflicted between your goal and a habit or response that does not support your goal. The best way to discover these opposing forces is to **Check Your Mind**, which we will address next.

Get Organized - Step Three

The last component of your resolution success model is to **Check Your Mind** - often. This action will keep you from getting lost, as you travel towards an organized life. As with any journey where you consistently check directions to ensure you are getting closer to your destination, **Checking Your Mind** should be the most often used tool throughout the day.

- When constructing your **Guiding Principle**, **Check Your Mind** to discover what and who you honestly think and feel is important.

- **Check Your Mind** to separate your Authentic Self from your Consumer Self.

- In any given moment, do my thoughts, words and actions support or oppose my ability to get organized and the values of my **Guiding Principle**? **Check Your Mind**!

- **Check Your Mind** to discover how you feel when expressing yourself in ways that that do not support being organized.

As we are all limited by the same 24 hours available each day, one of the greatest advantages of an organized life is efficiency. This means, *how* you perform your daily functions, has an enormous impact on what you accomplish and how you feel as a result. Managing oneself is crucial, as time is fixed and therefore not manageable. One characteristic shared by most people who have organized lives - *everything has a home.* Whether at home or work, your keys, wallet, purse, backpack, mail, clothes, accessories and paperwork should have a designated place where each one belongs when not in use. The built in efficiency is you know exactly where the items are you depend on most frequently. They are always at the ready, where you expect them to be and do not require wasting time searching for them.

Being flexible is also part of being efficient. So there will be times when you have a sound reason for deviating from your organization plan. As long as you honestly feel good about this change, rather than a weak justification for being lazy, then it is fine. However, if you act on an intellectual justification that you do not feel good about, your heart and mind will be out of alignment and undermine your success.

For example, during the day when no one else is home, I occasionally place my car keys, wallet and phone on the table next to the back door, rather than in their assigned *home* in the top side drawer of my office desk.

This action is a thoughtful strategy that employs a secondary, transitional *home* I use for these items when I know I will be leaving again within the next hour. It is simply more efficient for me. I only employ this strategy when no one else is home so these personal items do not interfere with the flow of other family members who may need to use that table for its intended purpose, which does not include my personal effects.

Your Resolution Success Model

Once again, the imagery you should have in your mind is a self-sustaining circle of success, driven and nourished by **Guiding Principles, Composing Yourself** and **Checking Your Mind.**

Spend Less / Save More - Step One

We will again use the same **Guiding Principle** used for weight loss and getting organized - "respect and love for myself and family."

Aside from yourself, who do you care about that would benefit from you spending less and saving more? Keep in mind, alignment between what you think and feel is the single most important factor. You need to honestly and authentically care about the people involved. If what you feel or do not feel is an expression of your Authentic Self, then it has to be right for you, in this moment.

Although the value of *spending less and saving more* seems obvious, take time to deeply consider all the ways this could improve your personal or business goals of helping not just yourself, but others.

Now consider how *spending less and saving more* will improve how you feel, decrease stress and give you a greater sense of control, freedom and choice in your life. Next, reflect on how these personal changes within you will add value and increase the level of happiness in the lives of the people you have connected to your **Guiding Principle**. The circle is now complete. You have created a self-reinforcing principle that will attract thoughts, words and actions to support your *spend less and save more* resolution. I am intentionally writing out *spend less and save more*, as these words are interpreted differently within the heart and mind, than simply saying *improve my finances* or *make more money*.

Caution! Resolutions primarily driven by benefits mostly fail because it emotionally disconnects the person from taking the daily action steps required to succeed. I think everyone desires the benefits of *spending less and saving more*, but do you honestly *feel like* taking the steps necessary to acquire those benefits? If you are being honest, many of you will answer no, you just want the benefits.

Spend Less / Save More - Step Two

Compose Yourself. You will need 3 sheets of blank paper for this exercise. On the first 2 blank sheets of paper, follow the general instructions for **Composing Yourself** previously stated.

With the 3rd sheet of paper, write your resolution, *spend less and save more.* Under your resolution write your **Guiding Principle** - "respect and love for myself and family." Fill up the page alternating your resolution and **Guiding Principle.**

As you do this, hold the image in your mind of the people whose lives will be improved (including you) and how that will feel as your financial situation improves. Also consider how your daily victories will feel as a result of having taken actionable steps to support your goal. Whether you accumulate money at home in a jar, envelope or safe, or at a financial institution, monetary goals provide the added advantage of being able to see the tiny, daily changes that usually go unnoticed with goals such as weight loss.

Emotion creates *motion*, which is why it is imperative to align your heart, what you feel, with your goal and **Guiding Principle. Composing Yourself** serves three purposes.

First, the "subconscious mind dump" helps remove reflexive behaviors in your subconscious that oppose you *spending less and saving more*. Second, it enables deposits to your subconscious that support the foundational habits of *spending less and saving more*. Third, it provides reinforcement of daily thoughts, words and actions to support how *spending less and saving more* improves your general perspective on life.

Let's look at another potent way to **Compose Yourself**. Write on a blank sheet of paper one action step to move you one step closer to *spending less and saving more*. Perhaps you bring your lunch to work a few times a week, not only saving money, but also addressing any health or fitness goals you might have. You will either plan or prepare your lunch immediately, or write down what time you will do it later that day. Now re-write your action step over and over, as fast as you can, until you reach the bottom of the page. If performing immediately, get up and do it - NOW!

Although your ability to *spend less and save more* will be challenged on a daily basis, each challenge provides another opportunity to succeed and feel good about that success. Spend some time thinking about your typical day and make a list of all your financial leaks. Bear in mind that while many daily expenditures might be small, the cumulative effect can be significant. Fortunately, this dynamic works both ways as the cumulative effect of small daily savings can also be significant.

Spend Less / Save More - Step Three

The last component of your resolution success model is to **Check Your Mind** - often. This action will help you stay on track *spending less and saving more*. **Checking Your Mind** should be your most frequently used tool to keep you connected to your **Guiding Principle** and help guide your thoughts, words and actions in support of your resolution.

- When constructing your **Guiding Principle, Check Your Mind** to discover what and who you honestly think and feel is important.

- **Check Your Mind** to separate your Authentic Self from your Consumer Self.

- In any given moment, do my thoughts, words and actions support or oppose my ability to *spend less and save more,* as well as the values of my **Guiding Principle? Check Your Mind!**

- **Check Your Mind** to discover how you feel when expressing yourself in ways that that do not support *spending less and saving more.* Are your head and heart in alignment with one another.

Your Resolution Success Model

As is true with the previous resolutions discussed, *spending less and saving more* should be associated with an image in your mind of a self-sustaining circle of small daily successes, driven and nourished by **Guiding Principles**, **Composing Yourself** and **Checking Your Mind**.

Well my friends, it is time to literally close the book on Resolution Solution 2015 and begin taking action!

Remember, your resolution might start in your mind, but can only be fulfilled when it mixes with your heart. It is the integration of the heart and mind that enables us to *feel like* succeeding in any lifestyle goal.

Visit me at ChrisWeiler.com to ask questions or get more detailed, personal guidance.

I Wish You All an Empowering Year!

About the Author

Chris Weiler is a performance expert to athletes, Fortune 500's and YOU! His background in philosophy, physics, and athletic development, inadvertently helped provide a foundation for his unique perspectives and processes in developing habits and behaviors to maximize personal performance in all areas life. He believes success in personally meaningful actions and goals helps contribute to happiness.

A native of Chicago, Chris enjoys his family, kayaking, rock climbing, 4 wheeling off-road, Buddhism, burning the midnight oil, problem solving and pie. His literary heroic thinkers are Isaac Asimov, Steven Covey, Aldous Huxley, William James, Steven Levitt, George Orwell, Ayn Rand, and Dr. Seuss.

www.ingramcontent.com/pod-product-compliance
Lightning Source LLC
Chambersburg PA
CBHW031334040426
42443CB00005B/334